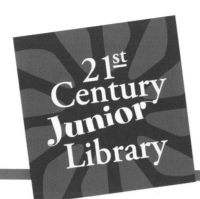

21st Century Junior Library

HEALING PLANTS

by Pam Rosenberg

CHERRY LAKE PUBLISHING * ANN ARBOR, MICHIGAN

Published in the United States of America by Cherry Lake Publishing
Ann Arbor, Michigan
www.cherrylakepublishing.com

Content Adviser: Paul Young, MA, Botanist

Reading Consultant: Cecilia Minden-Cupp, PhD, Literacy Specialist and Author

Photo Credits: Cover and page 4, ©Andreas G. Karelias, used under license from Shutterstock, Inc.; page 6, ©Ronen, used under license from Shutterstock, Inc.; cover and page 8, ©clarence s lewis, used under license from Shutterstock, Inc.; cover and page 10, ©Svetlana Privezentseva, used under license from Shutterstock, Inc.; cover and page 12, ©joanna wnuk, used under license from Shutterstock, Inc.; page 14, ©Rob Wilkinson/Alamy, page 16, ©Zeno Elea/Alamy; page 18, ©Damian Herde, used under license from Shutterstock, Inc.; page 20, ©Design Pics Inc./Alamy

LIBRARY OF CONGRESS CATALOGING-IN-PUBLICATION DATA
Rosenberg, Pam.
 Healing plants / by Pam Rosenberg.
   p. cm.—(21st century junior library)
 Includes bibliographical references and index.
 ISBN-13: 978-1-60279-278-4
 ISBN-10: 1-60279-278-X
 1. Medicinal plants—Juvenile literature. I. Title. II. Series.
 QK99.A1R67 2008

 581.6'34—dc22   2008014343

Cherry Lake Publishing would like to acknowledge the work of
The Partnership for 21st Century Skills.
Please visit www.21stcenturyskills.org for more information.

CONTENTS

Sunflower plants grow tall and have big flowers.

Plants for Many Purposes

There are many different kinds of plants. Some of them have pretty flowers. Others grow tall and leafy. Still other plants provide us with food to eat.

Did you know that some plants can also help us get better when we are sick? People have used plants to cure sickness for many years.

These plants will be used to make tea.

Some plants give us liquids that help our skin. Others have parts that can be used to make healthy teas to drink. Some plants are even used to make medicines. Let's take a look at some plants that heal.

Look!

Look for teas the next time you go to the grocery store. See how many different kinds of tea are on the shelves. Look at some of the labels. Were plants used to make the teas?

The leaves of the aloe vera plant are thick
and green.

Leaves and Flowers

The **aloe vera** plant grows close to the ground. It has thick green leaves. The leaves have sharp edges. A clear, thick liquid comes out when you cut open the leaves. Some people use this liquid to help heal skin problems. Aloe vera is also used to heal bad sunburns.

Chamomile flowers can be used to make a healing tea.

Chamomile is a flowering **herb**. Herbs are plants often used in cooking or medicine. Chamomile flowers have white **petals** and large, yellow centers. They can be used to make a tea. The tea is said to help people relax and sleep better. Some people say it makes their stomachs feel better when they are sick.

Create!

Would you like to grow a chamomile plant? Ask an adult to help you buy some chamomile seeds. Plant them in a container or in your yard. Make sure they have enough water and sunlight. Soon you will have your own pretty, white chamomile flowers.

The ginger plant is used for healing. It is also used to flavor food.

Stems and Bark

People use the underground part of the ginger plant. Though it grows underground, it isn't a **root**. It is really a special kind of stem

You may have tasted ginger. It is used as a spice in cooking. Have you ever eaten gingerbread cookies? Maybe you tried a drink called ginger ale.

Many people sip ginger ale when they have nausea.

Ginger is often used to help people who have **nausea**. Nausea means you feel like you are going to throw up. Ginger can help settle your stomach. Then you feel better.

Make a Guess!

Do you think your family eats foods that contain ginger? Guess one recipe that contains ginger. Ask the person who cooks that meal if ginger is one of the ingredients. Was your guess correct?

A medicine to treat malaria comes from the bark
of quinine trees.

Some plant medicines come from the bark of trees. **Quinine** is one example. It was the first medicine used to treat a disease called **malaria**. Malaria causes high fevers. People with malaria were glad to have quinine to help them feel better! You need a **prescription** from a doctor before taking quinine.

Ask Questions!

A **pharmacist** is a person who prepares and sells medicines. Do you want to know about more plants that are used for healing? Ask your pharmacist some questions the next time you are at the drugstore. She can help you learn more about medicines that come from plants.

Eating any part of the foxglove plant can make you very sick. It can even cause death.

Plant Safety

Many plants can be used to help people stay healthy. But it is important to remember that some can make you very sick. You can even die from eating certain plants. It takes a lot of training to know the difference between safe and unsafe plants.

Pharmacists can help answer your questions about healing plants.

Plant medicines are like any other medicines. Always ask an expert before using any of them. Doctors and other health care workers will be happy to answer your questions. They like using what they know about plants to help you stay well!

Think!

Do you know the names of some kinds of plants that are safe to eat? Hint: Grown-ups try to get you to eat them every day.

Did you say vegetables and fruits? You are correct! But remember, never eat something unless you know it is safe to eat.

GLOSSARY

aloe vera (AL-oh VAH-ruh) a low-growing plant with thick green leaves that have prickly edges

chamomile (KAM-uh-mile) a kind of flowering plant

herb (URB) a plant used in cooking and medicine

malaria (muh-LAIR-ee-uh) a disease spread by mosquitoes that causes high fevers

nausea (NAW-zee-uh) a feeling of being sick to your stomach

petals (PET-uhlz) parts of a flower that are usually brightly colored

pharmacist (FARM-uh-sisst) a person who prepares and sells medicines

prescription (pri-SKRIP-shuhn) an order from a doctor that tells a pharmacist what kind of medicine to give a patient

quinine (KWI-nine) a medicine that comes from the bark of a tree and is used to treat malaria

root (ROOT) the part of a plant that grows underground and soaks up water and minerals

FIND OUT MORE

BOOKS

Frost, Helen. *We Need Pharmacists.* Mankato, MN: Capstone Press, 2005.

Petty, Kate, and Jennie Maizels. *The Global Garden.* Cornwall, England: Eden Project Children's Books, 2005.

WEB SITES

Biology4Kids.com— Humans and Plants
www.biology4kids.com/files/ plants_man.html
Learn more about why humans need plants

Wonder Pets! Egg Carton Herb Garden
www.nickjr.com/shows/wond_ parents/wonder_crafts/wond_egg_ herb_garden.jhtml
For instructions on how to make an egg carton herb garden

INDEX

ABOUT THE AUTHOR

Pam Rosenberg is a former teacher who currently works as a writer and editor of children's books. She lives in Arlington Heights, Illinois.